DELIVERANCE 101

A GUIDE TO DELIVERANCE

Thank you for choosing Kayla Reese Ministries to educate you on deliverance. Deliverance 101 will help you develop, create, and enhance the "you" that has been in bondage.

By: Kayla Reese

Deliverance 101

By: Kayla Reese

ISBN: 978-0-578-82979-1

Copyright 2021

By Bloom Publishing, LLC

Scripture quotations are from the KINGS JAMES VERSION & AMP of the Bible unless otherwise noted.

Table of Contents

Chapter 1: What is deliverance and the importance of deliverance? 1

Prayer 8

Chapter 2: Soul Ties 10

Prayer 14

Chapter 3: How to administer and sustain deliverance? 15

Chapter 4: Know your authority 20

Prayer 23

Chapter 5: God is faithful to his covenant 24

Prayer 26

Chapter 1: What is deliverance and the importance of deliverance?

Ephesians 6:12 KJV

For we wrestle not against flesh and blood, but against principalities, against powers, against the rulers of the darkness of this world, against spiritual wickedness in high places.

Deliverance is being rescued.

Setting free is the release.

- There are times we are delivered but not set free. There is such a thing as being rescued but not released. Being rescued means I surrender what has had me in bondage; releasing is the repentance and rebuking.

- Think of evil spirits as pigs that have rushed into your house with mud, foul smells, slop, water, and drool. The kicker is that you invited some of them in, and some of them are the folk you allowed in your home; then, others are those that grew up with you. You don't want that filth with you or in your house.

- Sometimes it's not what you have done; it's what your parents and grandparents had opened their souls to, what they believed in and what they yielded to in the past. So it is imperative that you rummage into and through your family to see what things are present (diabetes, cancer, strokes, perversion, poverty, depression, or bipolar history). Look at yourself to identify what you battle with and then begin to ask questions. Examples: I feel so depressed and seeing my mother always down has me at a place.

- Demonic and evil spirits invade and dwell in bodies; they must have a WILLING host to operate. They come in through doors that we have left open, whether through sex, lies, manipulation, gossiping, or generational, to give examples. Demons are evil personalities; they are spirit beings. Their objectives in human beings are to attempt, deceive, accuse, condemn, pressure, defile, resist, oppose, control, steal, afflict, kill, and destroy.

Everything is NOT demonic; some things are opened to us, through not submitting or lack of discipline.

Self-discipline is defined as the ability to control one's feelings and overcome one's weaknesses, the ability to pursue what one thinks is right despite temptations to abandon it. (defined through Oxford Language)

(2 Timothy 1:7 For the Spirit of God does not make us timid but gives us power, love, and self-discipline.)

To be demonized is to be filled with demons, the spirits of darkness. Christians can never be possessed; they cannot be owned by demons because they are owned by God.

(1 peter 1:18–19, knowing that ye were redeemed, not with corruptible things with silver or gold, from the vain manner of life handed down from your fathers, but with precious blood as of the lamb without a spot [even the blood]) of Christ.)

(1 Cor. 6:19–20 What? Know ye not that your body is the temple of the Holy Ghost which is in you, which ye have of God, and ye are not your own? For ye are bought with a price: therefore glorify God in your body, and in your spirit, WHICH ARE GOD's)

Christians should always consider indwelling demons unnecessary and undesirable trespassers. A trespasser (the place of bondage) is one who is illegal upon the territory of another. Trespassers can only continue their illegal practices until they are confronted and challenged on the basis of one's legal rights purchased by Jesus Christ with His own blood. He has made the believer a steward over his own life. The devil has no legal right to him; however, it is up to him. The only time he has legal rights is when you have not repented; as long as you are in bondage and in denial, the adversary has legal rights to you.

1 Peter 2:9 But you are a chosen race, a royal priesthood, a dedicated nation, [God's] own purchased, special people, that you may set forth the wonderful deeds *and* display the virtues and perfections of Him Who called you out of darkness into His marvelous light

Being delivered or going through Deliverance is valuable. The process of expelling demons is called deliverance. Deliverance is not a cure for your bondage. YOU MUST DO THE WORK. Yet it is an essential component of what God is doing in relation to the current revival in the church. Some folk may say this is too much and some may say this is too little. No deliverance is the same; no one will go through deliverance the same.

How to identity that I need deliverance. (Some notes have been selected below from the Pigs In The Parlor, by Frank and Ida Mae Hammond)

- **Emotional instability**

  You always get emotional about everything. Sometimes it has nothing to do with you. You are just emotional. Examples of emotions include anger, continuous grief, hatred, depression, worry, insecurity, and feelings of unwantedness and unworthiness. These emotions build up in the presence of rejection, abuse, and no esteem.

- **Mental illness**

  Disturbance in the mind or through trauma in life, mental torment, procrastination, indecision, compromise, confusion, doubt, rationalization and loss of memory, insomnia. Mental illness can be generational.

- **Speech problems**

  Outbursts or uncontrolled use of the tongue, inclusive of lying, cursing, blasphemy, criticism, mockery, railing and gossip.

- **Sex problems**

  Recurring unclean thoughts and acts regarding sex. These include fantasy sex experiences, masturbation, lust, perversions, homosexuality, fornication, adultery, incest, provocativeness, and harlotry.

- **Addictions**

  The most common addictions are to nicotine, alcohol, drugs, medicines, caffeine and food. These develop after rejection, depression, lies, and deceit.

- **Physical Infirmities**

    Many diseases are physical afflictions due to spirits of infirmity (Luke 13:11). When the demons of infirmity are cast out, prayer is often needed for healing whatever damage has resulted. Thus, there is a close relationship between deliverance and healing. Miracles happen instantly, while healing occurs over a period of time.

- **Religious Error**

    Involvement in religious error to any degree can open the door for demons, objects, and literature from sources of religious error. They have been known to attract demons into houses.

- **False religions:**

    Eastern religions, paganism, philosophies, and mind science. Mind science is associated with yoga and karate, which cannot be divorced from heathen worship. You must annul the demonic contract you made.

- **Christian Cults:**

    Mormonism, Jehovah' Witnesses, Christian Science, Rosicrucians, and Theosophy. Some cults deny or confuse the necessity of Christ's blood as the way of atonement for sin and for salvation. They can also include some societies and social agencies, which will use religion (scriptures and God) as a foundation but on the blood atonement of Jesus Christ. They can be classified as bloodless religions.

2 Timothy 3:5 AMP

For [although] they hold a form of piety (true religion), they deny and reject and are strangers to the power of it [their conduct belies the genuineness of their profession]. Avoid [all] such people [turn away from them].

- Occultism and spiritism, séances, witchcraft, magic, Ouija boards, levitation, palmistry, handwriting analysis, automatic handwriting, ESP, hypnosis, horoscopes, astrology, divination... anything seeking supernatural from God is forbidden.

Deuteronomy 18:9-15 AMP

(9) When you come into the land which the Lord your God gives you, you shall not learn to follow the abominable practices of these nations. (10) There shall not be found among you anyone who makes his son or daughter pass through the fire, or who uses divination, or is a soothsayer, or an augur, or a sorcerer, (11) Or a charmer, or a medium, or a wizard, or a necromancer. (12) For all who do these things are an abomination to the Lord, and it is because of these abominable practices that the Lord your God is driving them out before you. (13) You shall be blameless [and absolutely true] to the Lord your God. (14) For these nations whom you shall dispossess listen to soothsayers and diviners. But as for you, the Lord your God has not allowed you to do so. (15) The Lord your God will raise up for you [a] prophet (Prophet) from the midst of your brethren like me [Moses]; to him you shall listen.

<u>Explanation of holidays</u>

Let's start with Halloween. This demon comes in through pumpkins and starts mesmerizing children. You give the demon of rivers access to your home, and this is their welcome sign. It is also a Jezebel. This spirit is identified not just through women but men as well. This evil spirit has been responsible for not only tearing down churches, pastors, and different Christian ministries but also breaking up many marriages, friendships, companies, along with getting many people to commit cold-blooded murders and suicides. When you celebrate Halloween, it brings forth 4–5 generations of curses and opens the door for the enemy to wreak havoc. Demonic costumes, no matter what they are, you are still in a covenant with the adversary. He changes your identity. You open yourself up to a whole world of the ruler of the kingdom of darkness.

Prayer

Lord Jesus Christ, I believe that you are the son of God and you are the only way to God. I believe you died on the cross for my sins and rose from the dead. I come to you now for mercy and forgiveness. I believe you have forgiven me and receive me as your child, and because you have forgiven me, I receive myself as a child of God. Lord you know the special problem I have, the demonic influences that torment me. Lord, I want to meet your condition and receive your deliverance. I forgive every other person, including those who have harmed or wronged me. I forgive them all now (name the person you need to forgive). Lord, I have forgiven everyone. I have laid down all bitterness, resentment, hatred, and rebellion. I also renounce every contact with anything in Satan's territory. I repent for being on that territory and I renounce it now. Also, if there is a curse resulting as a consequence of my involvement, I command the curse to be reversed. I thank you that on the cross you hung that I might be redeemed from the curse and receive the blessing. I claim that now I am released from the curse and I receive the blessing now! If I come against any evil spirit that occupies any area of my personality, I want to tell you that I hate them. I consider them enemies. I will not compromise with them. I will not make peace with them. They have no more place in me. I turn against them and in the authority of the name of Jesus Christ, I command them to leave me, I expel them right now, in the name of Jesus AMEN.

It is important to refrain from speaking in tongues during deliverance. Speaking in tongues is for you. Also, when you say Amen, do not pray, just receive the deliverance. Amen means, I allow the deliverance to begin

Chapter 2: Soul Ties

Soul ties are defined as a mystical bond between two people or you and another desired thing. A soul tie [FS1] is a concept to justify an ungodly relationship. We see that soul ties are not just a man and woman relationship. It is also known to be when you are entangled or when you have made a covenant with another other than God. You can be soul tied to people, food, yourself, relationships, jobs, money, family, and cars. They are idols. You have placed them as gods over your life. They are considered holds. Humankind is a composite of three distinct components: body, spirit, and soul. It contrasts with the bipartite view (dichotomy), where soul and spirit are taken as different terms for the same entity (the spiritual soul).

The Bible teaches that we consist of body, soul, and spirit: "May your whole spirit, soul or psyche (Ancient Greek: it means 'to breathe'), which comprises the mental abilities of a living being (reason, character, feeling, consciousness, memory, perception, thinking, etc., and body be preserved blamelessly at the coming of our Lord Jesus" (I Thessalonians 5:23). Our material bodies are evident, but our souls and spirits are less distinguishable.

The Greek word for spirit is pneuma. It refers to the part of man that connects and communicates with God. Our spirit differs from our soul because our spirit is always pointed toward and exists exclusively for God, whereas our soul can be self-centered. The joy, comfort and peace of God's presence can only be experienced through our spirit.

Sexual and Relational Soul ties

Sex is a tridimensional experience of spirit, soul, and body. Sex is one of the most common ways to develop soul-ties. We respond to sex as if it's ok; sex is not defiled when you are married. There are times when you have sex, even with the wrong spouse, it brings soul ties to things. Many times when you have sex with someone, you will find yourself saying "they made love to my soul" This is because they do; if you open yourself up to sin, you are able to be filled with demonic spirits. If you are battling with depression and the man or woman you are having sex with is battling depression, the spirit magnifies. You will find yourself wanting to commit suicide because the spirit grew. Look at this in the book of **Genesis 3:3.** It was a snake that tempted Eve. Also, in the book **Revelation 13:5-8,** it grew into a dragon. How big is your dragon?

Relationship connections

If you are married, going through issues, or in a relationship, you both should go through deliverance. Why?

You will still have the residue from your previous on you, and you will begin to connect yourself and fill yourself with things that will be tied to your soul.

After a divorce, you should wait at least 1 year before you get involved with anyone. This is written in counseling. The psychiatrist states the same; they recommend that you begin to work on your brokenness to ensure your next relationship does not repeat itself.

When you are married, be sure that you release the divorce in the courts of heaven [FS2], some folk are still married in the heavens and cannot move forward because you are still connected to the person in the heavens.... This goes forth with any relationship you have built sexually, emotionally, and so forth. Marriages that were not ordained by God are still active in heaven, through your vows made at the altar. Your vows make it legal in heaven. When you divorce through repentance, it breaks the legal rights in heaven. You have to petition the courts of heaven and plead your case. You have to petition the courts of heaven when you are divorcing not just soul ties but any spirit that has attached themselves.

While everyone's soul is fully active, not everyone's spirit is, because when Adam fell, the spirit died and was separated from God. Only in Christ is the spirit reconnected and reconciled: **"At one time you were separated from God. But now Christ has made you God's friends again ... by his death ... " (Colossians 1:21–22) (AMP).**

When you are connected to other folks, you begin to feel what they feel, and you experience what they experience.

The consequence of not being delivered from previous relationships

(just to name a few)
- Loneliness
- Bitterness
- Anger
- Divination
- Repeated cycles
- Perversion
- Masturbation
- Fornication
- Homosexuality
- Lesbianism
- Loss of identity
- Rejection

- **Soul-tie with your job**

When God tells you to leave your job, you develop so many emotions connected to the place because you have been tied with them for so many years. When you finally leave, you still feel the pull to go back, so you begin to ask yourself if you made the right decision. When leaving, you must ask God to disconnect you from the job to help you move forward. What keeps us there is financial stability, dependency upon other gods, fear, and rejection. All of this comes up when you are battling with leaving one job for another or leaving a job for setting your own business. It doesn't matter whether you are stable financially. You will begin to miss the relationships.

- **What keeps me from leaving my job**

    Poverty
    Fear
    Relationships
    Lack of wisdom
    Lack of understanding

- **Soul-tie with food**

    Depression
    Anxiety
    Obesity
    Deception
    Rejection
    Seduction
    Molestation

Prayer

Father, forgive me for connecting my soul to ungodly folk and things. Father, I dismantle and release every painful memory of the soul ties I have made. I break and divorce the soul tie with control, manipulation, lies, and divination. Father, from this day forward, I break this connection I have opened. Every relationship, whether it be through marriage, dating, or courting, I break the soul tie. I break the soul tie to things I have allowed to enter in through my emotions, mind, will, and soul. I break every ungodly soul tie I have allowed and that was forced. Father, I rebuke the devour that is attached to the soul tie. In Jesus' name AMEN.

Father, cleanse me with your love and release Your blood. Father, thank you that your grace has brought me again. Now come into my life and take over; fill every room in my house. In Jesus' name, AMEN.

Chapter 3: How to administer and sustain deliverance?

Can I deliver myself?

Yes. You cannot keep yourself free from demons or sustain from evil spirits until you begin to walk in this dimension of deliverance.

Philippians 2:12 (AMP)

Wherefore, my beloved, as ye have always obeyed, not as in my presence only, but now much more in my absence, work out your own salvation with fear and trembling.

If you have not gone through repentance, there is no way you can deliver yourself. Only believers can deliver themselves.

Isaiah 52:2

Shake thyself from the dust: arise, and sit down, O Jerusalem: loose thyself from the bands of thy neck, O captive daughter of Zion.

The range of temptations binding the believer is limitless, depending on what you open yourself up to.

The person can take themselves through deliverance by being taught how to do so. You ask, how is that a person can deliver himself? As a believer (and this is our assumption), he has the same authority as the believer in the deliverance ministry. He has the authority in the name of Jesus. And Jesus said it clearly, promising them that believing in my name, they shall cast out devils. Also, the retaliation to the casting out and the deliverance is overwhelming and will make you react vs respond.

With self-deliverance, you can loosen yourselves from any control of darkness (Isaiah 52:2)

What will keep you from receiving deliverance?

We often hurry to skip into the binding and loosening, speaking loudly and demanding the spirits to come forth, and nothing happens. You must speak with the authority you have, according to Mark 16:17, casting out demons in His name. His name has not only the power but the authority.

Curse
Sin
Pride
Passivity
Ungodly soul-ties
Occultism
Fear
Embarrassment
Unbelief
Lack of desire
Unforgivingness
Lack of knowledge

Doing self-deliverance or any sort of deliverance requires patience. Deut. 7:22 says God drives out spirits little by little.

Exd 23:23-29 (AMP)

Will not drive them out from before thee in one year; lest the land becomes desolate, and the beast of the field multiply against thee.

Steps to deliverance

- **Repent** - turn from your wicked ways, ask God for forgiveness, ask for forgiveness and for the posture of a sincere-hearted place.

- **Renounce**- begin to rebuke the sin or the thing that had you in bondage. Divorce the thing that had you in prison.

- **Release** - take what you renounced, and release it back to the pit of hell.

- **Restore**- for every unclean place you released, put in something good to fill the empty space again. Remember **1 Peter 5:8 Be well-balanced (temperate, and sober of mind), be vigilant *and cautious* at all times; for that enemy of yours, the devil, roams around like a lion roaring [in fierce hunger], seeking someone to seize upon *and* devour.**

How to maintain self-deliverance and gain self-control

(some notes are taught through the Deliverance Manual)

Proverbs 25:28 He who has no rule over his own spirit is like a city that is broken down and without walls.

- **Thoughts:** change what you think; you can no longer think of the place you were living in bondage. Remember you were bought with a price. **1 Corinthians 6:20 (AMP) You were bought with a price [purchased with a [a]preciousness and paid for, [b]made His own]. So then, honor God *and* bring glory to Him in your body. Philippians 4:8(AMP) For the rest, brethren, whatever is true, whatever is worthy of reverence *and* is honorable *and* seemly, whatever is just, whatever is** pure, whatever is lovely *and* lovable, whatever is kind *and* winsome *and* gracious, if there is any virtue *and* excellence, if there is anything worthy of praise, think on *and* weigh *and* take account of these things [fix your minds on them].

- **Appetite:** Change your appetite by changing your friends and surroundings; you are what you eat; if you eat junk, you will attract junk. **Proverbs 23:2 (AMP) For you will put a knife to your throat if you are a man given to desire.**

- **Speaking:** Your language must change; you must learn to speak the way freedom speaks and know how Kingdom talks. When we have conversations that are hateful, degrading, or gossipy, they sends signals to demonic realms that open demonic portals. They are called word curses.

- **Sexual character- 1 Corinthians 9:27 (AMP) But [like a boxer] I buffet my body [handle it roughly, discipline it by hardships] and subdue it, for fear that after proclaiming to others the Gospel *and* things pertaining to it, I myself should become unfit [not stand the test, be unapproved and rejected as a counterfeit].** The very thing that I am free from, I am released from

- **Emotions-** Don't succumb to overly emotional moments that will hinder you from gaining momentum.

- **Temper-** work on how you respond **Proverbs 14:29 (AMP) He who is slow to anger has great understanding, but he who is hasty of spirit exposes *and* exalts his folly.**

How to maintain and gain self-control

For when you were slaves of sin, you were free regarding righteousness. But then what benefit (return) did you get from the things of which you are now ashamed? [None] for the end of those things is death. But now, since you have been set free from sin and have become the slaves of God, you have your present reward in holiness and its end is eternal life.

- Get into the Word of God daily. Study, Study, Study.

Romans 6:20–22 (AMP)

- Find a healthy and positive group to join, whether in the church or outside the church. A church or a social group that will hold you accountable for the change.
- Pray-praying helps you live a submitted life.
- Use the gifts of discernment every moment that you encounter folk and things.
- Apply the blood of Jesus on your family and over your family.
- Fasting and praying consistently is the way you must keep demons and evil spirits out. **2 Corinthians 10:5 (AMP).**
- Keep your mind daily **Romans 2:12 (AMP).**
- Remember that you have power and authority **Luke 10:19 (AMP).**

How to increase or get to the next level

1. Know who you are
2. Operate in the current place
3. Live a submitted and clean life daily
4. Learn self-control
5. Learn self-discipline

Chapter 4: Know your authority

Repent

Jesus' first command to the people was "Repent"; he came to restore the Kingdom. He wanted to extend his invisible kingdom and its government to its earthly place.

The original plan was to do this through an agency through this plan. That's why God created you. That's why He said he called some to be, that means we are the agencies on the earth too.

God wanted to extend his wisdom and authority inside of man and that is the reason why the scripture says He created man in his own image. Every time he speaks, he deposits more into you. He doesn't pour or deposit more until you release.

To be his representation of who he is.

Genesis 1:26–30 (AMP)

26 Then God said, "Let us make humankind in our image, in the likeness of ourselves; and let them rule over the fish in the sea, the birds in the air, the animals, and over all the earth, and over every crawling creature that crawls on the earth."

27 So God created humankind in his own image; in the image of God, he created him: male and female he created them.

28 God blessed them: God said to them, "Be fruitful,

multiply, fill the earth and subdue it. Rule over the fish in the sea, the birds in the air and every living creature that crawls on the earth." 29 Then God said, "Here! Throughout the whole earth, I am giving you as food every seed-bearing plant and every tree with seed-bearing fruit. 30 And to every wild animal, bird in the air and creature crawling on the earth, in which there is a living soul, I am giving as food every kind of green plant." And that is how it was. 31 God saw everything that he had made, and indeed it was very good. So there was evening, and there was morning, the sixth day.

John 10:19 (AMP)

Behold, I have given you authority to tread on serpents and scorpions, and over all the power of the enemy, and nothing shall hurt you.

The word **dominion** is defined as seizing control over a territory. In Hebrew, this word means to rule and govern and to manage and master.

What kind of government does God want us to be? He created each of us to be kings and priests. **King**- ruler, is the executive branch of the government.

dom- quality

When the Redeemer came, all of your sins were taken away. When you repent, the old things are passed away.

One of the reasons we can't operate in the Kingdom is because you are still in sin.

I am given Kingdom access, power, and faith through repentance.

He has to trust you to give you more. You can pray all day and believe that you can do more and think that you can do more, but if God does not trust you, He is not giving you more.

Luke:10:19 (AMP)

Remember, I have given you authority; so you can trample down snakes and scorpions, indeed, all the enemy's forces; and you will remain completely unharmed.

Execute the judgment of the people on the earth, deal with the right of the people through the law, and the Bible teaches that God did not come to destroy the law but fulfill the law

He gave us the power to subdue the earth; you are to rule and dominate the earth. God wanted us to do this and still wants it,

When you are deceived, you are being ruled and governed by Satan.

Ephesians 6:11(AMP) Put on God's whole armor [the armor of a heavy-armed soldier which God supplies], that you may be able successfully to stand up against [all] the strategies *and* the deceits of the devil.

Every day, you should don the full armor of God. Donning the full armor of God is like putting on your natural clothing. It is your daily protection.

When knowing who you are as a Kingdom citizen, you don't and won't have issues with folk attempting to make you conform to the demonic ways. According to **1 John 4:4 (AMP) Little children, you are of God [you belong to Him] and have [already] defeated *and* overcome them [the agents of the antichrist], because He Who lives in you is greater (mightier) than he who is in the world.**

Prayer

Father, today, I repent for not coming to you sooner. I repent for shying back and allowing fear to keep me out of your power, authority, and safety. Father, I rebuke the devour that was set for my life and my age. Every unhealthy relationship that I have put before you, that is and has been attached to my soul, I detach it and believe that it has already been done.

Chapter 5: God is faithful to his covenant

Covenant is defined as an agreement.

God is faithful to his covenant. What is God's covenant?

Understanding the God covenant

John 8:36

So if the Son liberates you [makes you free men], then you are really *and* unquestionably free.

We can rely and trust God's covenant because he is committed to it.

- You must be committed to the covenant; your commitment keeps you at a place where you surrender.
- You must commit to your freedom; this commitment keeps you free. Stay at the posture of a YES. I remember a saying, "If you don't stand for something, you will fall for anything." Indeed, this is the truth. The covenant is His word. The covenant is HIM. Learn God-talk.
- You must learn the difference between God's voice and yours.
- **Ezekiel 1:28**: Like the appearance of the bow that is in the cloud on the day of rain, so was the appearance of the brightness roundabout. This was the appearance of the likeness of the glory of the Lord. And when I saw it, I fell upon my face and heard a voice of One speaking.

- **John 10:27** The sheep that are My own hear *and* are listening to My voice, and I know them, and they follow Me.

When God's mercy flows through us, then comes healing.

It's God's covenant of mercy that extended the benefits.

My purpose, however, is to teach the truth of the covenant positively, demonstrating from Scripture that it is the truth.

The covenant of God with His people is a unique relationship of intimate fellowship in mutual love. That was the covenant announced to Adam and Eve in the garden immediately after the fall. That was the covenant established with Abraham. That was the covenant as administered to Israel, even though Israel's covenant was burdened with the law. This is the nature of the perfect form of the covenant with believers and our children in the present, gospel age.

Hebrews 6:13

For when God made a promise to Abraham because he could swear by no greater, He swore by Himself.

God is the highest of anything; He made a covenant with himself; if he made a promise to Himself and he honored what He made with himself, then we are to keep it as well.

The new covenant makes God's mercy available for us. Because we have a covenant through the blood of Jesus and as believers, mercy is extended to us. Remember, we are healed and delivered through the blood of Jesus because of the death, burial, and resurrection.

Prayer

Father, thank you for allowing me to come and be delivered. As I have released every heavy burden that I was carrying through what was legal to me and to what was generational, today I dedicate my life back to you. I come out of my agreement with the enemy that was made through every family member, my disobedience, and my sinful ways. Come into my life again. Father, I receive you as my Abba (Father).

Thank you for trusting Kayla Reese Ministries with your life and setting your soul free. For additional services that Kayla Reese Ministries offer, please visit the website at www.kaylareeseministries.com

Kind Regards

Prophet Kayla Reese

www.ingramcontent.com/pod-product-compliance
Lightning Source LLC
Chambersburg PA
CBHW070108100426
42743CB00012B/2697